A POETRY COLLECTION

SKIPPING ROCKS
ON WATER

•

A POETRY COLLECTION

SKIPPING ROCKS ON WATER

•

CHET DIXON

TWEED

OGHMA CREATIVE MEDIA

www.oghmacreative.com

ISBN: 978-1-63373-396-1

Interior Design by Casey W. Cowan
Editing by Diana Ross
Interior Photos by Aimee Dixon Plumlee
Interior Drawings by Tex Edwards

Tweed Press
Oghma Creative Media
Bentonville, Arkansas
www.oghmacreative.com

ACKNOWLEDGMENTS

●

THANKS TO MY EDITOR, DIANA ROSS, for her professional help. I want to thank my daughter, Aimee, for making suggestions, asking good questions, and typing each poem. If it were possible I would also thank every individual in person who enriched my life with their presence and nurture. They kept me alive and moving forward, and have impacted my writing immensely. Many individuals have influenced my life and work with their love, companionship and encouragement to experience this great and wonderful world that offers us freedom to live, grow and express our feelings, passions, visions, hopes, and dreams. Thank you all.

Pebbles shine
Where clear waters flow
And wait in silence
When torrents rage.

Then when tempers cool
And waters clear
They come back shining
As if on stage.

When you skip a pebble
With a clear message in mind
And watch it sink
With its purpose intact,

Don't harbor anger
Or cry in shame.
Repeat the gift
By sending it back.

AUTHOR'S NOTE

•

HAVE YOU EVER WATCHED CHILDREN skipping rocks across smooth reflecting water? They find just the perfect thin rock that will hit the surface again and again before sinking. They use all their skill to sling it across the water counting each touch of the surface. Each touch of the rock and water makes a different set of splashes and waves, slow ripples, and then goes away. Writing poetry is much like skipping rocks on water. Each poem you release to readers makes a different splash and lives its own life. Some skip only a few times, while others seem to skip on and on. I have skipped many rocks and have written many poems and keep searching for that perfect one that will be a perfect skipper. Whether I find the perfect skipper or not, as a poet I will go on listening to each whisper in my mind, hoping that when it has been transferred to words, it will skip.

FOREWORD

•

AS CHET DIXON GREW UP, he spent most of his free time along the beautiful and pristine White River of Missouri and in the deep woods of the Ozarks. It instilled a deep desire to capture both its beauty and music for the soul. His desire to write about its romance and adventure led him to write his first poem in 1950 when he was only 12 years old. Hundreds of poems later, his first collection of poems, *Beyond the Trailhead*, was published in 2016. That collection clearly revealed a deep love and understanding of the great outdoors. *Affections Not Sleeping* was published in 2017.

When Chet was a young boy there were special places that he found inspiring. He would visit them often, in secret. One special place required that he slip out of the house at night and walk through dark woods to his favorite bluff lookout high above the White River and listen to the rumbling water as it flowed over rocky shoals. Those times at the lookout, he would explain later in his life, inspired him to become a writer. These experiences gave him an open door to imagination and expression never before known to him. It created a great desire to share with others the beauty and tranquility of the Ozarks backcountry.

From his early years and on through his professional career, his poetry writing increased over time capturing different parts of his life. Now, in 2018, this new book, *Skipping Rocks on Water*, reflects a wide ranging view of his life and experiences common to most of us. His hope is that it will help readers remember their life and what is important to them.

This is who Chet Dixon is. I know him well because he is my Dad.

Aimee Dixon Plumlee

CONTENTS

•

Dedicated to all my loved ones whom I hold dear in my heart.
Thank you for inspiring me to become who I am and will be.

the

POEMS

•

What you skip may be a dream
But skip it into the passing stream
Even if it seems weak and pale
Skip it... it's your gifted trail

SKIPPING ROCKS

•

When I tried to skip a rock today
I thought it would easily skip away
But to my unpleasant surprise
It went down in sudden demise
Not defeated another rock was thrown
And just as quickly it was gone
Another and another I threw
Just to see what they would do
Then I watched one hit the water
Delighted it almost made me totter
It hit and skipped away
As if on air and wanting to stay

A simple lesson that day I learned
Before another defeat returned
Keep doing your gift and never cease
It's something sacred to release
Like rocks on water is an unlikely pair
Yet together produce a gift to share
Gifts are to be given away
Not to be hoarded to stay
And when its purpose is secure
Unselfishly given to keep it pure
You are skipping your sacred treasure
Allowing others to know its pleasure

What you skip may be a dream
But skip it into the passing stream
Even if it seems weak and pale
Skip it—it's your gifted trail

LIFE

•

Our lives will never stop moving
Even when we hide away.
There will always be hills to climb
Because the valleys are here to stay.

That's why we climb to the summit
Of every hill we need to climb
For there's nothing worthy below
In the valleys left behind.

Life keeps us needing to climb
No matter how young or old.
It's the valleys, hills and summits
That will define the lives we mold.

PEACE

●

Peaceful places are graced
By the Father above
That are given freely to guard,
Nurture and to love.

We must never take for granted
Their tranquil but fragile souls
And always bless the Creator's
Blessed, sacred goal.

MEMORIAL

•

The dark granite wall lay stoic in fluid blue
Shadows spread upon wooden rails.
Walker milled with quiet endless stares,
Giving and taking gifts and cares.

Captured by its reflection they say few words
Trying to connect pieces of past and present.
Not knowing how, they give honor humbly,
With heavy hearts, they gaze numbly.

With hushed voices some stand in salute
Among the givers, receivers and scorners.
But all hearts stood or sat touching,
Fluid blue names, with tearful mourners.

DUST ON MY FEET

•

I'm never swayed by side streets entering.
They may look great but often centering
Upon a way not meant for me.

I'll never fear the changes coming.
With all my might I'll keep on running
Toward the light I see.

The dust on my feet may keep building,
And the stress doesn't keep my soul from filling
With the peace God freely gives.

Now I'll shake off the dust without meaning.
The task will be hard but atoning
For a life of freedom that lives.

WILDERNESS MOMENT

•

When I walked along a meadow today
A soft voice met my ear.
It was sweet and sent from heaven
For anyone needing to hear.
It said, "When you walk in my woods
You will never be alone.
I will be with you during the storms
And remain after clouds have gone.
Then when the sun shines brightly
And the grasses wave gaily on the glade.
I will be closely beside you watching
Sharing the wonders for you I made."

CHANGE

•

When desperate times tower before us
And action has almost disappeared,
One man can move despair to opportunity
And can change the world,
If he acts.

HOTEL

●

Trail-less words and laughter rise
As crowd nests swarm.
My words grow still and numb.

The evening deepened as
Spirits made lewd gestures.
Words became nothing, grotesque.

Unnoticed I slip away
Beneath evening lights and stars.
I found a gentler sound.

Far from the crowd
The evening I sought
Lingered within me.

Troubles lifted.
My soul found its rightful place,
Unshackled.

A BUG IN MY SALAD

•

A beetle wiggled in my salad and
Gently lifted a lettuce stem.
In this friendly gathering I mused
Should I kill or just eat him?

I'm not so sure he wanted to be here
Well-disguised in my salad bowl.
I could just use my fork to smack him
Or just pick him up and swallow whole.

I began to think about his life
And what I'd like him to do.
What if he found me in his feast
Or swimming in his stew?

How could this friendly bug
Have safe retreat?
Oh yes! I'll just pick him up
And drop him at my feet.

So once upon the wooden floor
I knew he would sprint away.
However, he tried to climb my leg
As if he wanted to stay.

So what must I do to solve my dilemma
And save this little guy?
I can hide him in my napkin
And much later say goodbye.

THE CROWD

•

This chatter sounds like ten thousand jesters and elated women,
Visiting.

It feels meaningless, like the sound of wild geese
Running aimlessly.

My mind becomes jelly
Reacting to shock—
Shivering inside.

I waste away—

I am alone—

I wish you were here!
The crowd would not matter any longer.

THE HEALING WOODS

•

Into the healing woods I ran
Where crowds were far way,
Where sunshine, snow and rain
Cleanses with nature's play.

Where senses feel the touch
Of forest smells and taste
Inside the healing woods
Where spirits quietly wait.

Along the fields by crystal streams
Where quail and meadowlarks sing
I feel so loved and blessed and
Share the healing songs they bring.

LOBBY CREW

•

One could be less
Than part of a lobby crew,
Watching people come and go
Milling like expectant cows,
Wanting but not pleased,
Gazing at distant vacancies
And pushing words self-destructible.

One could learn less
Than being with the standing,
Staring, and waiting gang,
Waiting for some imagined
Or familiar face not appearing.

One could do less
Than pretend to be occupied,
Never seeing the evening news,
Hotel books, and magazines
Disguising intent.

One could do much less
Than talk with a lobby tongue
Even though it may be less
Than a normal thing to do.

NEW START

•

What should you do
When you experience shame?
Don't hide in fear.
Own it and shun placing blame.

Even if the wrong
Has left an indelible mark.
Humbly ask for mercy,
Then hurriedly make a new start.

FRIENDS

●

Let the forest grow
Tall and dense
Even if to many
It makes no sense.
Let the acorns fall
To cover the ground.
Make each seed rich
And each one found.

Then as my friends
Find evening treasure
That nature supplied
With heavenly pleasure,
I'll hide in secret
But not to harm,
To watch God's world
And majestic charm.

Then without a sound
I'll slowly slip away
Filled with wonder
And wanting to stay.
But they and I
Have places to go
Our destinies are different
Among friends and foe.

But for a short while
Our spirits are at rest
As they fed on acorns
And I, their hidden guest.

L I F E

•

In life we are often broken
Then healed in due time.
We sometimes need to retreat
But still persevere.

Life takes us through storms
Then gives us blue skies.
It leaves us with its stars
To show that healing is near.

Life makes us stand tall
When troubled waters surround.
It offers its healing
That's beyond profound.

Life beckons us to lead
And sometimes follow along.
It tolerates our self-importance
And lifts us when down.

Oh, Lord, You know our good and bad
And gives us lasting grace,
I hold my cup up high to You,
And toast Your marvelous face.

MY DREAMS, MY JOURNEY

●

I can sit and wait
At the starting gate
Or get up and begin
To conquer my fate.

I can keep on hoping
That my dreams will appear,
Or begin my journey
And conquer my fear.

I can begin very soon
To get my win
Stop looking back
Wanting to begin.

As I get older though
I keep thinking about dreams
Yet knowing so well
I'm running out of steam.

When I'm really being honest
I know it's getting late
I keep getting older
And I haven't left the gate.

I know I'm getting older
And my dreams are beginning to fade
Though weak and frail
I must accept the bed I've made.

I'll never completely lose
Those dreams of long ago.
I must begin my journey
That only I can know.

My dreams, my journey
All belongs to me.
So, I'll just hobble on my way
Where I should already be.

CREATION TIME

•

When ink dries up and pens grow silent,
Nothing has gone to sleep.

Sometimes a pen has nothing to do
When creation is stirring deep.

Developing words may grow like mosaics
Waiting for foundation blocks,

Stones that are firm, strong and clean
Like sounds of townhall clocks.

The creation wait may not be long
Or could keep me waiting and fearing.

It will mix events, thoughts, and space
Before my ink starts reappearing.

I'll just bravely wait while considering a truth
That I can never change.

It's the fear that creation's mysterious nature,
Has chosen to rearrange…

Everything.

POEM

•

Every poem that takes my ink
Has tried to capture the truth, I think.

Many who read them may question my quest
I say read on friend, it's my very best.

Nothing is lost when honestly trying.
To find a nugget before lost or dying.

Every poem is a winner and nothing lost
When sharing its lessons at very little cost.

STRAYS ALONG THE MAPOCHO

•

Dingy street lights flicker as daylight disappears,
Streets and alleys are deserted, and still.
Anxious children emerge like rats hunting
For cast away treasure, unwanted.
Hidden in Mapocho tunnels and deserted buildings
They hide with subconscious eyes and ears open.
Then slipping from hiding like thieves,
Avoiding snares and unwanted pests,
They enter an unknown evening.

When strays unveil and leave their tombs
They vigilantly look, listen, and assay needs
That compel them to act out their chore.
Some scatter like scavengers prowling
For scraps, discarded, unsightly, and unwanted.
Others beg, steal and pick pockets
Since charity seldom is found.

Dusk transitions to another order,
Day life sleeps, night awakens.
An endless schedule moves in routine fashion,
One tranquil, undisturbed, the other
Distressed and clamorous.
Days and nights remain the same,
Precarious and doubtful.

Sleepless and un-kept
With unsettled stomachs growling,
Their night search begins
For things lost and abandoned.

while competing, without aggression
Strays search and prowl their territory
Like street dogs of Santiago
Looking for a treasure to survive.

Music and laughter often float
From beyond walls where kings dine.
The revelous sounds glide across
The cool evening air.
Imaginations stir with thoughts of fine dining,
Dancing, and dreams of wine, silk pillows and furs
And joyous sleep as heavenly sounds
Float from deep inside the private lives
With restful nights, fulfilled.
The truth stings.

Are we all strays of different breeds.
Some free and greedy,
Others lost, sleepless, afraid,
But discarded, unclaimed and helpless,
Co-existing with affluence and privilege?
Could survival of the fittest be right where winners
Take their spoils and deserve better,
Believing their greed is justified?

Too soon the order changes.
Strays quietly return to their tombs.
Dining has ended.
Sleep may come again soon.
The routine never ends.

MASTER

•

When tossed about
To and fro
Not knowing which way to go,
Just know that
God is there.

Look up
To heaven above.
There you will find
His fortress—love—
is everywhere.

D R E A M S

•

I can easily observe,
Learn, and have a dream.
But alone it quickly fades,
Wilts, and dies.
I can watch it creep away
Without one blink,
Or fear,
Or just as easily
Help it live
And let its heart appear.
But there is something
About a dream
That demands unfailing hope
Or it loses its value
For lack of the dreamers
Will to cope.

DON'T THROW AWAY TOMORROW

•

Don't throw away tomorrow
For reasons clear today
Tomorrow can be much greater
No matter what blocks our way.

Don't throw away tomorrow
Its gift we must receive,
And when it comes tomorrow
Its value we must believe.

Though doubts and troubles linger
When tomorrow finally begins,
We can know a friend is with us
And whose promise we can depend.

He walks with us in sunlight.
He is with us when it's dark.
We need not fear what's coming,
Or tomorrow's new start.

Our todays are all experience
Their lessons may be slow to appear.
But experience is always teaching
And its lessons we need not fear.

FORGIVENESS

●

Grasping a mask to hide
I am lonely
And afraid
I am alone
And helpless

The world around me is empty
Pretenses consume me
Secrets hide me
Dishonesty shields me
Disguises cover me

Naked I hide
Broken
Rejected
Lost
Unforgiven

Seeking transformation
I knock
I beg
I feel helpless
I listen

The door opens
I see light
I hear a voice
I understand
I am forgiven

HOPE

•

When pain lies hidden
Beyond my hands and words
When lost and confused
In a deep dark place
When the world so loved
Seems devoid of love and grace
I find myself crying
And my spirit dying
Without hope.

Obvious or disguised
My healing is in reach
There is always a path
Through disaster and grief
Soon there will come
A sense of relief
To help me stop crying
That tells me I'm not dying
Without hope.

I seek help in the forest
And along clear rivers
Where I can catch a cool breeze
And feel the shivers
Then is when I know
That something will deliver
Help for my crying
And prevent the dying
And give me hope.

SOARING

•

I wait to soar among clear heavens,
Among the eagles, unafraid.
I need the wind beneath my wings
And a hope in my heart.
Let me see Your face unshielded
And hear Your voice aloud.
Lead me as I follow closely
And teach me to never part.

When You are with me
The universe opens wide.
And through Your loving grace
You always hear my call.
So let me soar among the eagles,
Trusting the promise You made
That with You near
I will never fall.

L I G H T

•

Light sends away the dreaded dark
To cure every hurt and snare
Light is sent with special power
With all God's love and care.

Light heals the abandoned broken hearts
And reveals the robber's snare,
When danger threatens to block our way
God's light is always there.

Light wets our ravaged, dusty world
And gives the rain to make things grow.
We need not fear the darkest times
Just stand without fear and know…

God's light is always there.

W I L D E R N E S S

•

The wilderness never obeys me
Nor tells me how to act.
Its unique nature always prevails
And never holds anything back.

You find God in the wilderness
Hovering all around.
In the wild, you feel His presence
As you listen to every sound.

In the wilderness, you hear His spirit teaching,
You bask in His perfectness.
In the wilderness God is easily found,
And there He chooses to bless.

In all its natural wildness
and as its stillness and harshness unfold,
They who trod a wilderness place
Its splendor they'll always hold.

PRAISE

•

I am a minute speck of dust and
You, my Lord, all love and grace,
Why be so attentive of me?
Why should you choose to care, and
Even more, to share
A love that sets me free?

Who am I, my Lord, among the stars
That you should love and want
To take my cares away?
And if I never understand,
One thing I know for sure.
Inside your loving care I'll stay.

I am so small in your universe,
An unknown fragile matter
That took a breathing life.
Even small, without worth,
You hold and keep me safe
As I walk through worldly strife.

As a servant of yours, my Lord
I shall never stop to rest
Without an act of praise.
As your servant I'll stand in awe
Of your marvelous heavens and earth
And my hands to you I raise.

A SOARING SHOW

•

Black vultures gracefully soared nearby,
Coming close without a sound.
From my bed of leaves and stone
I knew I'd not be found.

As they gracefully traveled on silent air
I marveled aloud.
There could be no better place
To hide away from this soaring crowd.

Here among the cliffs I sailed with them
Where few will ever know
The joy of riding their silent glide
With eyes transfixed upon their marvelous show.

MY DEAREST

•

You appear with every new coming day
And soar with the morning breeze.
You sing my favorite songs
From springtime rains to autumn leaves.
Every time we walk on trails of old
Where you set my feet on stone,
My dreams of you will never die
Until my last breath is gone.

WILDERNESS MOMENT

•

The voices of the wild
Are worthy of reaping
They speak to the soul
And comfort the weeping
Along cool streams
In the breezes from the hills
The voices of wild places
Speak softly and still
Come, sit on my chairs
Rest will soon appear
Miracles you will find here
Through listening, laughing and tears
Capture it quickly
Unattended it will disappear
Treasures you will find free
There is no need to fear

SONG

•

My soul awakens
When church bells ring
At the beginning
Of each new day
Their lovely melody
Touches my heart
Their messages
Come to stay
To me they speak
A song of praise
To the greatest joy
And peace God gives
They tell me
That all is well
And that today
I can begin to live
I praise your wondrous
Name my Lord
You lift me up
In every way
Lord give my feet
A higher plane
A place for me
To safely stay
You are the only
Thing I need
Down here

Or up with You
Tell me Lord
Guide me Lord
In whatever
You have me do
Tell me Lord
Guide me Lord
In whatever
You have me do.

G I A N T

•

The giant ambled toward the herd
Others kept safely behind
As I sat observing with wonder
Quietly hidden in my blind

For sure he had taken his rightful place
Among his selected herd
I could only watch in awe
Not saying a single word

Two options quickly came to mind
As I watched in hunter fashion
I could harvest this monster
Or draw upon compassion

To my surprise I found a kinship
To this beast on a wilderness stage
His power of beauty and grace
Was given from experience and age

Soon he took away his herd
To safe places they always go
Then I reviewed my history
Learning I was more than a foe

SECRETS

•

Go with me now
As the sun goes down
We can dance and play
As shadows creep
Then when stars stop hiding
Secrets can be told again

As the night passes
We can sit and listen
To night creatures
Living what we miss
Finding what we lost
And hiding still

If morning finds us
Huddled warmly
And the new sun
Reflecting a melody found
Let it ring through the trees
And down the valley floors

Then when it crosses
The lush green fields
And enters the town gate
Run with it
Into the prison of love
While secrets live on

PART OF LIFE

•

Life is
feeling a cool breeze after a summer day
viewing a thousand vistas from my feet to the distant horizon
hearing chirping birds in fields and along my bluff
observing children playing in the heat of competitions
seeing soaring eagles and vultures floating in updrafts
watching the red and grey foxes eagerly searching for a meal
feeding friendly deer and turkey then watching them and
falling to sleep as raindrops play music on a tin roof
This is part of life

Life is
feeling the pain of a deceased, long-lasting friendship
seeing a wildfire ravage a stand of virgin pine and fir
feeling helpless as snow and ice melt and seas rise
hearing a baby's cry when its mother cannot return
feeling the earth violently shake beneath your feet and anxiously
anticipating aftershocks
hunting for a lost plane somewhere on land or beneath the sea
listening for a call for help but unable to bridge the gulf to rescue and
watching war dismantle and destroy the lives of young men and women
This is part of life

Life is
accepting risk as normal but growing to fear it
being a strong caregiver to being cared for as a child
knowing where light is shining but unable to walk out of the dark
moving from proactive, to reactive, to inactive, unwillingly

realizing the necessity of lifelong choices then finding it easy to ignore them
giving up control and power to a growing desire for safety and security
being praised for excellence then relegated to something old, outdated and obsolete
and living with purpose
being persistent and patient to becoming unsure, weak and dependent
This is part of life

Life is
having courage and hope and facing sunshine or storms
when you know the deck is stacked against you—you never stop
putting hope in the place of despair and defeat
giving help without knowing the who or why or how
teaching what you know to others so they can grow beyond you
writing and talking about honorable values and virtues and
walking unclear trails to provide safe passages
waiting for the sunrise to cure the aches of dark times
fighting the fear of losing while struggling to hear the victor's song
praying with no doubts that your prayer is heard and
submitting to the call of your heart and honoring your time and space on earth.
This is part of life

Life is
joy, comfort and beauty
it is pain, fear and disorder
it is created new then grows old and
it has a spirit born of courage and hope that
can transform the torn and worn body and ravaged soul to live
and forever journey forward

All this is part of life

RAGE

•

The raging silence of the soul
Will often escape the languages we know.
Entering fearlessly and strangely waiting
It creeps on forward not abating.
But we know that beyond this storm awaits
Soft west winds and friendly mates
Steering by faith through raging times
Onward to calm shores that courage finds.

WINTER'S SPELL

•

Snow keeps falling soft and quiet
All through the night
Growing deep as cedars weep.

All wild things hide away
To safely stay
Until this winter storm again turns warm.

I will not run from this stormy night
Hiding I'll huddle out of sight
And quietly and carefully watch.

Surely Spring will melt this cold
And these chills will fold, and
I can tell of this dreadful spell.

On and on all wild things sleep
As snow grows deep, but
On my perch I begin my search,

Looking for a time when life appears
As springtime nears and life returns
And this long winter's spell adjourns.

LIGHT

•

Light sends away all dark
So it cannot hurt us more
He sent us light to show a path
That we could not see before.
The light will lead us on
To a safe and heavenly place.
Then at the end when time is gone
Our souls will abide within His grace.

EPITAPH

•

This life I've had has been a
Great treasure. It has given me
More than I could ever measure.

After years of living and
Learning there is nothing to
Regret, because this gift of
Life is free from debt.

All I've ever done was do
My very best and leave
The verdict to others whether
I passed the test.

WESTBOUND ON 66

•

Travelers keep going, never stopping
Vision fixed upon their goal.
Lodges waiting for their guests
Hoping luck will fill their roll.

Eyes of travelers strained from gazing
Needing beds and dinners hot
Moving onward following dreams
Tired, worn, but not ready to stop.

Sunlight dropping, stars appearing
Travelers begin a search for sights
Of something special on 66,
The magic of flashing neon lights.

Then begins their anxious talking
And getting closer they begin to laugh
Knowing soon their legs can walk
To stretch their tired, aching calves.

Eager to see the city limits
Its magical, glowing, moving lights
Travelers now in strange surroundings
Search for restful dreamy nights.

Later on, an alarm clock sounds
They hurriedly take breakfast waiting
It's time to go and hit the road
It's getting late and daylight's wasting

Away they go on down the highway
Where cars and trucks are all a mix
Going somewhere in a hurry
On the endless Route 66.

DREAMS

●

Your dreams may fizzle a thousand times
Before they rise to fly
People may say you're just a fake
And that all your dreams will wilt and die
But in the heart of every dream
Grows a bond of courage and will
And out of the shadows quietly appear
Something living with life to fill.

To many your dreams are idle folly
A waste of a useful mind
But a miracle lies just beyond each thought
Ready to take its place in time
So fizzle or fly, just dream on
Even when the whole world fails to see
That you have the courage and will to live
To unshackle and set your dreams free.

S E L F

•

There's power in being yourself,
Imitating others you can't go far.
Trying to stand in another's shoes
Is much like chasing a star.
Keep taking yourself to places
Where you have never been.
Only there, discoveries and mystery
Will never, never end.

LESSONS

●

Dark came early to the slopes
Clouds in eerie flight surround
All sights below dissolve from view
As I hover in a shelter found.
The barren forgotten landscape
Showed no intent to notice or share
Its firm vice grip to earth
As it held a solitary stare.
Far below campers slept
With familiar things close
Here in wild surroundings
Nature was my unconcerned host
On through nature's spell
My stay could only wait
With no control of time and place
And no escape.
Looking back I feel relief
And sense of lessons learned
My life is okay anywhere
Though some dangerously earned.

UNIQUE

•

This creature I am is so carefully made
And my hands are proof to show.
I can only be what God has made
And there's nothing more precious to know.

I am an original brand of my own
And never a copy or replica made.
My voice, my mind, my soul is unique
Being myself I should never be afraid.

We must be who we were made to be
And dare to follow our unique design,
Living that uniqueness with fervor
Proudly revealing we're one of a kind.

Hurry on now, and be what God created
That's all you are allowed to be.
It's time now, it's getting late,
The world is waiting for the "you" to see.

THE ROOT

•

My mind is pulled
By fevered hope
That I would change
And someday be,
More than what I discern
And know
About my assumed
Destiny.

Travels have taken me
By foot and head
Making choice a prize
That I can take.
But the other end
Of my destiny
Is firmly set
When brought awake.

FUMBLE THE BALL

•

When you get old, my young friend,
You begin to fumble the ball.
You get things all mixed up
And inevitably fall.
Your "thinker" gets too fast
For the rest of your game,
And sometimes, you find
That results are far from the same.
When young, stout, and robust
You knew you could pass any test.
But oh! Now that you are old
You often fail doing your best.
I must admit the league I play
Is not what it used to be.
I show up for the game though
Even when no one's there but me.
When you get old, my friend,
You often fumble the ball.
But where I've been
And what I know and do
May be far ahead of you.

SONG

●

I thought everything in life was right
But in the middle of the night
The storm came rushing in

It seemed that all was lost
And now I would pay the cost
But a small voice said to me

"I am here
You have nothing to fear
I've been here all along

Oh, don't you hear My voice
Just listen
And rejoice"

Soon the storm had almost ceased
And all around me joy released
As I felt the Master's touch

He said, "My son why be bound
When My love is easily found
Waiting at the open door?"

"I am here
There is nothing to fear
I've been here all along

Oh don't you hear my voice
Just listen
And rejoice"

Now Lord, I lift my hands to You
Your love is beautiful, kind and true
And now I give You all my praise

In Your presence my burdens lift
Oh what a Savior, what a gift
I give You glory and praise

Oh Lord, You are surely here
There is nothing to ever fear
And You've been here all along

Lord I hear Your lovely voice
I'm listening
And I'll rejoice

Yes, Lord, You are here
There is nothing to fear
You've been here all along

Lord I hear your lovely voice
I'm listening
And I'll rejoice

LORD

•

Thank You Lord
Far more than words can say.
Thanks for keeping my life in touch
Within Your perfect way.

I can see Your shining face
Even when there's thorns and grief,
Because Your love rings with joy
And my soul there finds relief.

I know that I can have peace
That only You can give.
Within You my soul soars like hawks
Above the rims where their peace lives.

If I could see beyond the storms
Where Your peace resides,
My soul would hover closely, Lord,
And with You abide.

If I could feel Your promise
That peace is ever close and sure,
Then with my praise I'd lift Your name
And in this life all things endure.

But now, without a perfect view
I come to where You stay,
As everything I lay down
With trust You are my way.

I know so very well
That my source is completely whole.
I need not worry or feel so lost
I only need to listen for my role.

I'll be patient
And in all things persevere.
I'll be confident and assured
That good and truth is near.

GETTING OLD

•

Getting old is easy to define
And doesn't take much thought or time.
Old behavior is obvious on every side
Much different when young with nothing to hide.
I'm sure it's those spots of graceful gray
Or the shaky hand or sight beginning to stray.
Maybe it's the things I forgot to button, zip or comb
Or having to think awhile about how to get home.
I'm sure it involves what makes me man
Being strong, alert to lend a helping hand,
And how I treat my lover who never goes away
When she has reason to criticize me every day.
Maybe it's the way I walk in a bent watchful gait
Or the casual limp and sway making people wait.
Getting old is easy for me to define,
But I'd rather talk about it some other time.

GLADES

•

I raised my eyes and cocked my ear
And suddenly began to hear
The coming of night and change of guard
And west lights falling silhouettes marred

Robins were scurrying to cedar roosts
Owl began hunting and evening hoots
But I, I sat waiting as snows flew north
Their airstream mission bursting forth

Everything seemed busy in a singular way
Changing with change creeping its way
I sat still as night became dark and deep
Then soon left the hallowed place—
                    To let it live and sleep.

HIGH VIEW

•

Wherever majestic mountains stand
Whether near or far away
I always wish for more.
And far, far out beyond my view
I know there lies
New gifts and mysteries to yet explore.

But right now if I could make a wish
For all the things I need
And what I wish to be,
I'd wish that all through time
These mountain gifts be known and open
For all the world to feel and see,

How mountain vistas give a gift
That cures our failing sight
And heals the weeping soul.
But as we view its blemished face
I sense the need to make a vow
To keep it safe and whole.

So now I simply make a vow
With an open heart and mind
To save a treasure from demise.
And every time I share its peace
I'll write a script, a plea, a song,
To stir the minds of the simple and the wise.

WHAT WILL I DO?

●

When I see then all is dark,
Hear then all is silent,
Smell then all is scentless,
Feel then can't,
Understand, then all is confused,
Know order then all is chaos?

Must I be sad
And curse the wind,
Choose to be afraid
And hide?

Or should I remember
All I've learned,
Be thankful
And brave,

Thankful that I
Walked this way,
Even though times
Have surely changed?

It's all a choice
For each to make.
No one can guide or steer
The road we take—

Or the consequences,
Or fate.

SONG

•

Walking in the sunshine,
Soaking in the rain,
I'll keep on smiling
Even when I walk in pain.

Life may be short and bumpy
But God's peace breaks each fear,
Just keep walking in the sunlight
For heaven's peace is ever near.

Get up—don't sit down,
Shout to heaven,
Stand your ground.
He is the Good Shepherd.
He listens for your voice.
Never, never stop,
Be thankful,
And rejoice.

Be thankful
And rejoice.

The sound of songs and praise
Will pierce the darkest night
When devils begin to threaten
And you seem to have no fight.

The Master stands beside you
Ready to guide you home.
He's a shepherd that guards His flock
He protects when hope is gone.

Get up—and don't stay down,
Shout to heaven,
Stand your ground.
He is the Good Shepherd.
He listens for your voice.
Never, never stop,
Be thankful,
And rejoice.

Just never, never stop,
Be thankful
And rejoice.

DARE

•

Dare to dream
Dare to act
Share your hopes
Never step back
Plant a seed
A shade to spread wide
Always walk in light
Never hide
Though little you are
In a world so giant
Stand for right
Always defiant
Live in hope
With end in mind
Live as Christ taught us
To love and be kind.

THE GREYS

•

Feeding new babies is a
Full time chore, whether for
Deer, turkey, or the greys
At my door.

I'm told to not feed them, just
Leave things wild, but I've
Always had a weakness for
Beggars, it's been my style.

Maybe I need forgiveness for
What wrong I do, I'll
Not do it for long though and
Only for a few.

Again today, I'll feed them when
They come wild with desire,
And all the time I told myself
This action is not so dire.

But knowing what they say is true
I'll need to change my plan.
It will take a while to
Convince me even when I understand.

Now, I promise to quit this
Unkind act of hiding and observing
And let nature care for itself
Without my generous serving.

COUNTRY

•

Country life is better than money
Its vistas and smells are sweeter than honey
Country surprises declare its space
As people breathe deeply with smiles on their face
Cool evening breezes move through stoic trees
Nighthawks begin to talk as stars twinkle free
Galaxies sparkle clearly throughout deep space
As human spirits contemplate their rightful place
Country is a place where one can think and dream
A place where one can release their creative stream
Country creates vision and hope of heaven on earth
Fresh, clear and fragrant as a new blossom's birth

MOVING ON

●

When life seems filled with closing doors
And they become a prison of mind
They may even tell us, just go and hide
For there's nothing worthy to find.
But we know our lives are filled
With a piece of heavenly light
And if by chance we stumble and fall
We have the power to stand and fight.
So when we feel emerging grief
And thoughts of failure and blame
Look to the light in our journey's path
And know that life remains the same,

Just moving on.

A PRAYER

•

If You choose me Lord to do a job
That's okay with me
I know it's a duty I cannot shirk
Your servant I choose to be.

Your endless love so graciously given
May choose me to go or lead
In places so small yet profoundly great
To lift one soul in need.

Your gifts so wrapped in arms of grace
Wait for me to speak,
A word that only I can speak, and keep.
Yes, Lord.

WIND

•

I'm waiting for the wind
That only You can send
Then I can soar and fly.

I patiently wait, oh Lord,
Bring on the wind,
Then I can soar
In Your transluscent sky.

Bring on Your wind
To bear up my wings
For all the world
And masses to see,

That the power that's held
In Your hand and breath
Can soar like eagles
With me.

BAD TIMES

●

When the way ahead
Seems cluttered,
Unsure,

Carefully respond,
Stand tall,
Endure.

Stand back to where
The path is clear,
On track.

Start again with confidence,
To bring things,
Intact.

Sometimes your compass
May slip off course,
A ways.

Or you may be right
And should not doubt,
Or stray.

Stand tall and closely
Listen to your
Spirit's command.

Then what is really true
And right,
You'll understand.

Bad times have short lives
Unless you allow them
To stay.

Remember the good you have,
And know that time
Can usually clear the way.

INVISIBLE STEPS

●

Voices of the night
Crept into my path
I pushed them away
And they pursued.
Not until daybreak
Did I find my tracks
Empty of life,
And a gap
Between my mind
And death's facelessness.

PRAYER

•

Thank You Lord
For the infinite possibilities
You have provided my life.
Open my eyes
That I may see them clearly.

Open my mind
To know the difference
Between truth and illusion.

Let the choices
I make for my life
Be those You would choose
For me, my Lord.

And as I grow
In knowledge and wisdom
Help me follow You
And my actions
Bring glory and honor
To Your name.
Amen

MY SONG

●

As we walk along our path
To a future still unknown
The road will surely be bumpy
Unless we live our song

It will keep us going forward
Not faint or afraid
The path will be our own
And not some replica made

So now we must hurry along
And with faith will assure
That we will do our song
And prove we can endure

And on the day somewhere ahead
When our curtain begins to fall
We'll look at what we've done
And will clearly recall

That life goes just one way
A path that's worn by choosing
What should be done this moment
To prevent an act of losing.

ONE WAY

•

I must be getting older
Or just growing mature
The getting older is fine
But the other I must endure

Things don't seem to work now
Like they one time did
Something happened along the way
And time just came and slid

My ears don't seem to function well
Much like my eyes and hands
They all seem on vacation
And don't listen to my commands

Many even call me Sir
And it makes me feel unsure
Will I someday become helpless
Or will I always endure

Without a doubt I'll get older
And strange things will surely come
But as I keep getting older
I'll never turn and run

I'll just keep on going
Because there's obligations to keep
And I'll keep going all directions
Even wrong on one way streets.

CURVES

•

Unknown curves loom ahead
No one knows where they lead.
Will they meet my greater need
Or will there lie a curse instead?

Worry could be my strong reaction
Or I could wring my hands in fear.
I could even shed an anxious tear
Or wait for fate's retraction.

Even if curves give doubt
And my choices seem undefined
I'll plod ahead with an open mind
Unless I choose to turn about.

Beyond the curves there could be wonder
Waiting around the bend in the road.
Then I should shoulder the load
And embrace what I fail to ponder.

There may be beauty ahead,
Vistas, streams and waterfalls.
There may be pleading calls
To wake a mind that's dead.

God is our guide on every curve
When what's ahead is unknown.
These encounters will have come and gone
While connected to whom we serve.

GHOSTS IN MY PATH

•

Ghosts of youth,
Uninvited,
Often visit me,
Eagerly eating bones,
Lost,
In forgotten forests.

Even though paths
Are gone, I see them.
They hide
Under monster paws,
Sharp fangs,
And flashing eyes.

My soul before them
Lays bare.
The heat and cold burns.
Voices around me sing
Of ghosts
And old bones.

HINDSIGHT

●

After years of
Living and learning
There is nothing
For me to regret
The most wonderful gifts
This life has given
Were given completely
Free from debt.

But even if some parts
Of my life and deeds
Are not so pretty
For public display
I won't forget them
But will strive to do better
Looking to the future
For better days.

VOICES

•

In the nestling of the leaves
The voice of ages speak.
Listen closely, you can hear it
Speaking gently, calm and meek.

ALSO BY

CHET DIXON

BEYOND THE TRAILHEAD

AFFECTIONS NOT SLEEPING

CHET DIXON GREW UP IN the Ozarks backcountry. He was born in a log cabin built by his father and went to a one-room schoolhouse that had 12-18 students each year. He considers growing up in the country a rich background for his life of work and writing.

After growing up in the Ozarks, his desire to explore the world led to several universities and a diverse work history. In his early twenties, he worked with migrant workers in the fruit harvests of Oregon and Washington and served as a fishing guide on Missouri lakes and rivers. He later worked for city and state governments in leadership positions. He was also a consultant to the Missouri Women's Council of the Missouri Department of Economic Development. His work experience includes speaker, trainer, workshop leader, writer, strategic planner and consultant for personal and organizational change. He is a businessman and President of Ministries of Love, Inc., an organization that builds Christian schools in Chile, South America.

His publications include Learning, Changing, Leading: Keys to Success in the 21st Century, co-authored with Sue McDaniel, and with whom he has penned fifteen basic training documents used for consulting work with the Missouri Women's Council. Chet's first collection of poetry, Beyond the Trailhead, was published by Tweed Press in 2016, and was followed by his second collection, *Affections Not Sleeping*, published in 2017. This collection of poems, *Skipping Rocks on Water*, continues to portray his love of the great outdoors, especially the wilderness backcountry.